BEADS
THE ART
OF
STRINGING

$3.95

By Genie Ragan

Cover Design by Pat Patton

Illustrations by
Christiane Ragan
and
Pat Patton

I would like to thank
Cleveland C. Weil of
Lapidary International
Hobby City
Anaheim, Ca., for his
moral support and his
indulgence in my effort
to complete this work.

This work is dedicated to Lily Siow, the lady who taught
me to do stringing and knotting the Chinese way.

Published by Gem Guides Book Co.
3677 San Gabriel Parkway
Pico Rivera, CA 90660

CONTENTS

PEARL AND BEAD STRINGING

Once you have learned the art of stringing beads, you will find that you will be able to design and create strands of beads and pearls to compliment anything in your wardrobe or satisfy any whimsy. You won't have to settle for a necklace you don't really care for, just so you have some beads to match your new red dress. With just a little imagination you can combine colors, textures and sizes to design beautiful necklaces for yourself and for friends. You will be able to create new strands from old beads for an exciting, up-to-date look. Or you may want to restring that favorite necklace, if the string is dirty and worn. Whatever your needs, you'll find that knowing how to string beads will help you save high labor costs and satisfy your creative needs.

WHAT YOU WILL NEED TO GET STARTED

- Beading material: silk, nylon, tiger tail or monofilament
- Beading needles: flexible or English (rigid) type
- Crimp beads
- Bead tips
- Clasps
- Needle nose pliers
- White glue (Elmers glue)
- Beading awl, 'Tee' pin or hat pin
- Beads, beads and more beads.

Once you're started and doing a lot of stringing you may want to add:
- Head loupe (magnifier)
- Tweezers
- Beading board
- French wire (bullion)

You may not be familiar with some of the terms used or why you will use them, so it seems appropriate to explain them before going on.

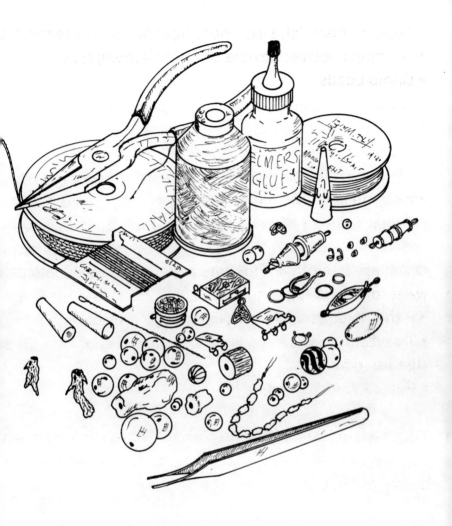

CHOOSING THE PROPER
BEADING MATERIAL

Beads and pearls come in all sizes, and the drill hole are also of various diameters. It will be your job to selec the proper weight cord for the beads, according to the siz of the drill holes and the weight of the beads.

Freshwater rice pearls will require a very fine silk o nylon, usually OO, O, A or B. Medium weight cord, C or D i normal for 4 to 6 mm. pearls. Colored stone beads an pearls measuring 7 mm. or larger will need heavy strin such as E, F, FF, or FFF. You may find that your supplie uses numbers rather than letters to designate the weigh of the cord, especially if you're buying nylon rather than silk. If this is the case, #1 is finest and #8 will be the heaviest.

SILK

Silk is available from suppliers in many colors, as well as black and white. It can be purchased in spools containing from 135 yards (FFF) to 925 yards (OO), or by the card with a needle attached. Cards usually measure 72 inches long. The cards are handy for occasional beading, but are more costly, and there are not as many colors available.

Silk is an all natural fiber, the strongest known. It is the most expensive beading cord, and is always used for fine pearls. It knots very well and drapes beautifully. Silk will stretch with wear, however, not as much as nylon.

As far as I can determine from the suppliers I deal with, silk is available on spools in twenty-eight colors, plus black and white.

Colors are available in weights E, F, FF and FFF. White allows us more choice in weight with OO, O, A, B, C, D, E, EE, F, FF and FFF. Black comes in D, E, F, FF and FFF. The colors and suggested uses are listed here, to help you determine colors you may need.

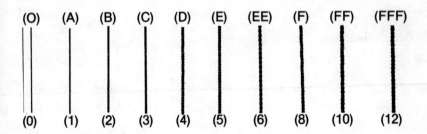

THE MANY SHADES OF SILK

WHITE . . . . PEARL

GREY . . . . SILVER BEAD

BROWN . . . . TIGER EYE

CHOCOLATE . . . . TIGER EYE

BEIGE . . . . PEARL

GOLD . . . . CITRINE/AMBER

BRIGHT YELLOW . . . . LIGHT AMBER

LIGHT GREEN . . . . JADE

BRIGHT GREEN . . . . JADEITE

MEDIUM GREEN . . . . PERIDOT

DARK GREEN . . . . MALACHITE

BLUE GREY . . . . GREY PEARL

AQUA . . . . TURQUOISE

NAVY . . . . SODALITE

BLACK . . . . HEMATITE/ONYX

CORAL . . . . RED CORAL

PINK . . . . PINK CORAL

STRAWBERRY . . . . ROSE QUARTZ

ROSE . . . . RHODOCHROSITE

BABY PINK . . . . RHODONITE

RED . . . . RUBY

MAROON . . . . GARNET

RUST . . . . CARNELIAN

LILAC . . . . LIGHT AMETHYST

VIOLET . . . . DARK AMETHYST

BABY BLUE . . . . BLUE LACE AGATE

COPEN BLUE . . . . BLUE ONYX

ROYAL BLUE . . . . LAPIS LAZULI

Silk on cards with the needle attached is available in white, in weights 1, 2, 3, 4, 5, 6, 7 and 8 (lightest to heaviest). Colors are limited to gold, dark green, lilac, violet, navy, baby blue, royal blue, red, maroon, pink and black. The weights available are: 2, 4, 6 and 8.

You may find additional colors and/or weights at your supplier, but these are the ones I am familiar with and it should be enough to get you started.

If you value your time and your beads, DO NOT USE COTTON OR POLYESTER SEWING THREAD OR DENTAL FLOSS. It simply *will not* hold up.

NYLON

Nylon is available in different weights and colors, though you will find the selection somewhat more limited than with silk. It too can be purchased by the spool or the card. Nylon knots well, and is as durable as silk. It drapes like silk, however, the colors are not usually as vibrant or 'true', and it stretches more than silk. You will need to pre-stretch nylon before knotting by hanging the strand over-night with a weight attached to the bottom end.

NEEDLES

The needle most often used is the flexible wire needle. It is a twisted strand of fine wire with a large eye. It is flexible enough to go through holes that aren't aligned quite right and they handle curves well. There is also the English type which is rigid. I have never had an occasion where the English type was needed, however, some people prefer them. Flexible needles come in four sizes: 6, 8, 10 and 12, with #6 being the finest and #12 the heaviest. The eyes are fairly large, so threading is simple. The eye will close on the silk when pulled through the first bead. They can be re-opened with a pin if needed, but usually the needle is discarded after each stringing is completed.

TIGER TAIL

Tiger tail is a steel strand coated with a clear nylon or plastic. It is somewhat stiffer than nylon or silk, so cannot be used for knotting or weaving. But it is often called for when stringing very heavy strands or Austrian crystal because the sharp edges of the drill holes will cut through silk or nylon.

BEAD TIPS

Bead tips are used for finishing the ends of the string and attaching the strand to the clasp ring. It is a small cup with a hole in the center of the bottom and a hook on the top which loops around the jump ring of the clasp. The cord is threaded through the opening at the bottom of the cup, then knotted. The knot will rest in the cup and the hook is then closed around the clasp jump ring. See illustration.

Another type of bead tip or knot closure, that is often used, looks very much like a hollow ball, cut in half and opened with the cord hole in the seam and a hook at the top for attaching the clasp. The strand is threaded through the hole, the hemispheres folded together over the knot, and the hook is looped around the clasp ring. See illustration.

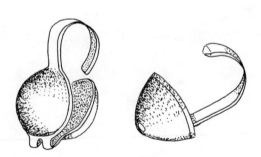

FRENCH WIRE
(BULLION)

French wire or bullion is a silver/gold plated hair-like wire, coiled very tightly to form a tube. It is the most elegant, professional finish to a fine necklace. It is the most difficult to master, and the most expensive. However, once you've learned this technique, and see the results, I feel sure that you'll see it's most worthwhile.

Silk ends are threaded through the French wire, then through the first bead to knot, forming a gold loop around the clasp ring. This adds security to the strand by protecting the silk from the friction of moving against the jump ring. It looks very nice when done well, like a loop of gold or silver connected to the clasp ring. Bullion is usually sold in three foot lengths and is available round or square in both white and yellow gold finishes to match clasps. Expect to pay about two dollars per foot. You will use approximately one inch for each strand, so a package of one yard will finish thrity-six strands.

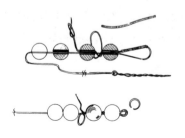

CLASPS

A clasp is anything that attaches one end of the necklace to the other whether it is a hook and eye or a karat gold, designer clasp paved with precious stones. The clasp should be chosen with care to suit the necklace. Light weight costume beads, may do well with a spring ring clasp, while heavy beads will require a screw-type barrel clasp. The filigree fish-hook type is most often seen of fashion beads and pearls. It looks nice and is quite secure for all but the heaviest beads. Most of these are found in precious metals (platinum, gold and silver) as well as the plated or gold filled type. Clasps can be very costly or as inexpensive as a few cents each. The choice is yours. Security should be the primary factor in choosing the right clasp. But don't overlook appearance. The fastener should blend into the necklace, unobtrusively, or it should compliment the strand. Fine pearls are often finished with designer clasps set with stones and worn to the front of the neck for a dramatic look of elegance.

NOTE: The ring attachments on your clasp or fastener, must be soldered shut if you are using silk or nylon. You would be amazed at how quickly a strand of cord can find it's way through even the tiniest opening in a ring.

CRIMP BEADS

Crimp beads are little rings used with tiger tail or monofilament, for finishing and securing the ends. The tiger tail is threaded through the crimp bead, through the clasp ring and looped back to thread through the crimp bead again. Needle nose pliers are used to squeeze the bead flat on the tiger tail to hold it tight.

BEADING BOARDS

Beading boards are wood or plastic boards with grooves for laying out the beads when a pattern of spacing is required, or for graduating beads. There is an outer rim to keep the beads from rolling off while you work with them. The beads are first laid out and the pattern arranged on the bead board. Changes can be made and the beads rearranged easily, and the finished strand visualized before going onto the string. This is really a great help when you are combining different colors and sizes, since you must maintain a pattern. Re-graduating loose pearls is much easier with the aid of a beading board too, especially if it is the type with a bead gauge incorporated in the grooves. The board may also be marked in inches for measuring the length of the necklace.

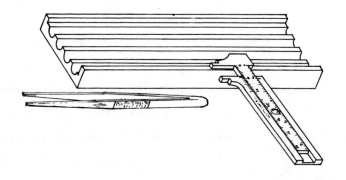

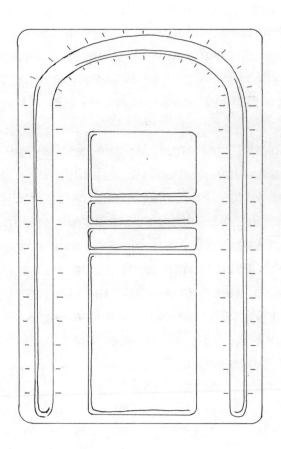

HEAD LOUPE

A head loupe is a magnifier worn on the head by jewelers and others who require magnification of the work while keeping both hands free. The lense can be moved above the eyes when it is not needed and back when you desire. The holes in beads are very small and a magnifier can relieve the strain on your eyes when you do beading or other close work.

Another type of magnifier works the same but attaches to your eyeglasses instead of having a head band. You may prefer this type if you wear glasses.

BEADING AWL OR 'TEE PIN'

A beading awl is a small handle with a very slender, tapered end which comes to a point. It is used for encouraging knots into place, and also for removing misplaced knots. A beading awl is also useful in clearing out the holes in beads if it is blocked with silk or glue.

A 'tee pin' is used for the same purpose as the awl. It is the pin used for securing a wig to the wig form and looks like the letter T. If you don't have a beading awl available this will work well in it's place, though it is not as comfortable in the hand.

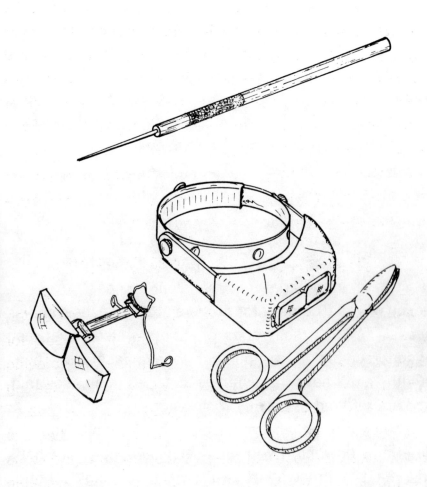

HOW MANY BEADS YOU'LL NEED

Generally speaking, beads are sold on temporary strands or 'hanks' of monofilament, in 16 inch lengths. A clasp will add anywhere from three-quarters of an inch to one and one-half inches to the strand, and knotting will add another one to two inches for each hank used. Don't forget to allow for this when designing a new necklace.

The lengths you will most often see are:

bracelet	7 inches
choker	16 inches
princess	18 inches
matinee	24-26 inches
opera	36 inches
rope/lariat	48 inches

You will also come across others in 28-30 inches, and on occasion, 60-72 inch ropes or lariats which have been added recently to compliment todays fashions. These lengths don't have trade names as far as I can ascertain, and are referred to only by their length.

When you purchase your beads by the hank, you can determine how many you will need very simply. One hank will make a bracelet of two rows or a single choker, unknotted or a princess length, knotted. Two hanks will make a matinee length and a bracelet or one knotted opera length, and so on.

If you are working with loose beads, you may have to do some calculating to arrive at the right number of beads to use. The beads are measured in millimeters, however, the length is measured in inches. It would be a lot easier if the length was metric also, but we have to adjust to inches. There are approximately twenty-five (25) millimeters to each inch, therefore, you multiply the number of inches by 25. A sixteen inch strand would measure 400 mm approximately. If you are using ten millimeter beads, divide by ten and you'll arrive at forty beads. If six millimeter beads are being used, divide by six and so on, according to the size of the beads used. If the beads are to be knotted in between, allow for the knots, and don't forget the clasp and attachments. A beading board is a big help here since everything, including the clasp, can be laid out and measured first.

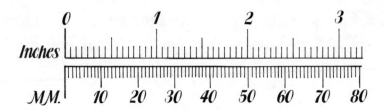

USING TIGER TAIL

Now you understand terms and the materials you'll be using and you're ready to start stringing, right? Well, let's try some costume beads and get you going.

Your first project will require:

- tiger tail (six inches longer than the finished necklace).
- clasp
- two crimp beads to match the clasp color
- needle nose pliers
- beads

Thread one end of the tiger tail through the crimp bead and through the clasp ring. Now double the tiger tail back down through the crimp bead, and crimp it flat, first from one side and again from the other side to secure it, using the pliers. Make sure it is as tight as possible all the way across. Clip the tail end as close as possible to the crimp bead, or you may work the end down through the beads if the drill hole allows. Now thread the beads onto the tiger tail from the loose end. After the last bead, another crimp bead is added. Go through the clasp ring and loop back through the crimp bead, just as you did at the beginning. Work the tiger tail until you move the clasp down close to the beads. Now flatten the crimp with the pliers from one side and then the other. Clip the tail or thread it back down through a couple of beads, and then clip. That's it! You've created your first necklace, and I'll bet it wasn't nearly as difficult as you may have expected. Imagine your feelings of pride when people compliment the strand.

Here are two tips:

Always pull the strand tight enough to make the beads bunch up somewhat, in order to eliminate gaps. The beads and the strand will relax after you've finished working with them and the necklace will smooth out.

Make sure there is no tail of monofilament or tiger tail sticking out of the beads. Even a very tiny tail, only a fraction of an inch, can scratch the neck and be quite irritating.

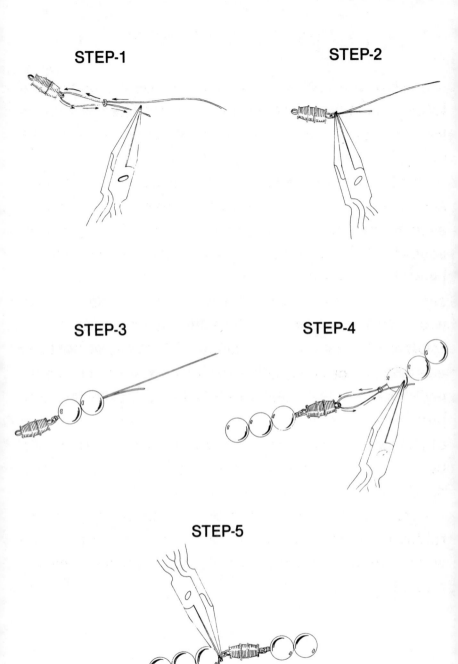

STEP-1

STEP-2

STEP-3

STEP-4

STEP-5

20

CLEANING PEARLS

The next project will be using pearls on silk (or nylon), so we will digress here for a moment and discuss the cleaning of pearls, which must be done BEFORE they are restrung.

Pearls are organic gems, made up of calcium carbonate, and they are very sensitive to acids, even mild acids such as that found in wine and vinegar. NEVER use ammonia or any jewelry cleaner that contains ammonia, for cleaning pearls. There are commercially prepared solutions especially formulated for the cleaning of pearls, which work very well and will not harm the nacre layer.

DO NOT use hair spray while wearing pearls, and don't use perfume or cologne where the strand will lie on your neck. Dab perfume behind the ears instead. The acids in perfume and hairspray, will destroy the outer (nacre) layer of the pearl, and it will 'die', losing all it's luster and beauty. Once a pearl 'dies', there is nothing that can be done to restore it. Prevention is the only answer.

Pearls that are slightly dirty should be cleaned by rubbing carefully, and individually, with a damp washcloth. If pearls are cleaned after each use, they will retain their luster.

Discoloration occurs when oils from the body are allowed to remain on the pearls and the oil collects dirt. This requires restoration. The pearls should be cleaned or restored ON THE OLD STRING.

Soak the strand in warm water with some mild liquid soap, or "pearl cleaner" for about fifteen minutes, to soften the dirt and oil. Now, brush gently with a very soft brush (an old toothbrush works well). Make sure to cleanse the entire pearls, especially around the drill hole. Rinse in clear water and pat dry with a soft towel. If the pearls still look dulled or yellowed from age, you should soak them for fifteen to twenty minutes in "20 volume" peroxide, undiluted, and still on the old string. After twenty minutes, the peroxide will stop working, so there's no reason to soak any longer than that. Rinse in clear water and pat dry. Hang the pearls in the air, or in the oven if it has a pilot light. The string will draw the moisture out of the holes so they may dry inside completely. Don't rush the process. Give it a day or two if necessary. Moisture left in the holes will cause the new silk to rot and break in short order and you'll find yourself having to restring the whole strand again very soon.

If you can, you may want to hang the pearls in the sun to dry, since the sun will help to bleach them back to their original color. This is as far as you can go in the restoration and if this doesn't clean them, you will have to take them for refinishing and polishing by a lapidary or pearl house. Expect to pay a fair price for this service, it involves a lot of time, expertise, care and patience. Fine pearls are well worth this expense. You will never be able to replace them for the price of refinishing. If you still cannot justify the cost, then you will just have to accept your heirloom pearls for what they are and learn to love their golden hue.

USING SILK OR NYLON

Let's assume that for this project you are using graduated pearls or beads. If they are on an old string, leave them there and save yourself some headaches. Remove them, one at a time as you thread them onto the new strand. If they are loose or the old string is broken, lay them out on your beading board. Start from the center with the largest pearl and work out to the ends, using an equal number of the same sizes on each side, from largest to the smallest. You'll find that most strands will graduate a certain distance across the front of the necklace and the last four inches on each end are uniform. A strand may be sharply graduated or very slightly. The normal procedure is a sharper graduation in fashion beads and less graduation in pearls or fine necklaces, with perhaps a one-half millimeter (½mm.) difference in the front and only one-fourth millimeter (¼mm.) graduation to the back, until they become uniform at the ends.

You will need:
- one fish-hook type safety clasp
- two bead tips or knot closures to match the clasp
- a flexible needle
- silk or nylon

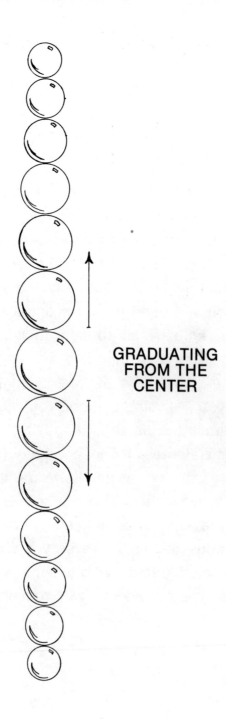

GRADUATING
FROM THE
CENTER

Each inch in length, translates to one-half inch in the fall (where it lies on the neckline) of the strand. In other words, if a sixteen inch strand falls about one inch higher than you would like, you will need to add two inches in actual length, for it to drop to the desired length.

When measuring the silk for a necklace, you will need a doubled strand, if you are using a spool. Carded silk or nylon, is doubled and twisted already. If the strand is to be unknotted, you will need a length equal to the finished necklace, plus an extra six to eight inches, for the ends, doubled. If the strand is to be knotted, you will need two and one half times the finished length DOUBLED. Therefore, if you are using a spool, you will need a single strand, five times the finished length of the necklace. A princess length (eighteen inches), will require about ninety inches of cord. Once on the needle, you will have a double strand of forty-five inches. This will be plenty for knotting and tying off the ends. If you are using carded silk, you will use only forty-five inches, however, you should never cut the silk off the card. Use the whole length and then cut the strand. That way the needle will remain attached for future use.

Unwind a length of silk, two and one-half times the finished length of the strand. Thread one end of the silk through the needle eye and double it. Knot the two ends together and saturate with white glue. Thread your needle from the hook end of the bead tip through the hole and pull the knot down into the cup. Now add your pearls, one by one, pulling slightly on the strand to eliminate any possible gaps between the beads. After the last pearl is on the string, thread your needle through the bottom (cup end) of another bead tip and move it tight against the last pearl. Clip the silk about four inches beyond the bead tip. Now, separate the two strings, tie a knot, pulling it snug into the cup and add a drop of glue. Tie again and work some of the glue up over the knot or add another drop of glue. Allow the glue to dry. Now you can clip the tails at both ends.

To attach the clasp, hook the bead tip to the ring on one end of the clasp and bring the hook down to form a loop. The end of the hook should rest inside the rim of the cup so there is no gap for the ring to pull out. Now repeat the procedure at the other end of the clasp or connector. If you use needle nose pliers, closing the hook on the bead tip around the clasp ring will be very simple task.

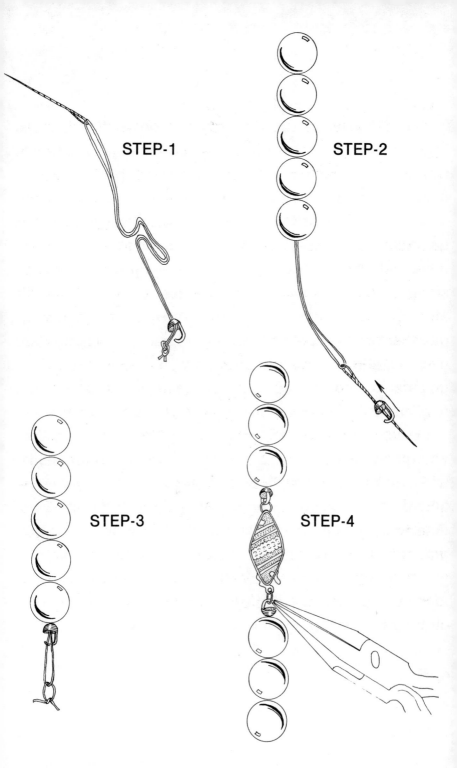

STEP-1

STEP-2

STEP-3

STEP-4

One thing to note here, regarding the bead tips or knot closures. They are available in both large and small, and need to be chosen according to the weight of the silk being used. The hole in the bottom of the cup must be just small enough to hold the knot in the string. Fine silk will slip right through the hole in a large tip, and on the other hand, heavier silk won't even pass through the hole of a small tip, nor will the cup accommodate the knot. You will also want to match the color of the crimp bead, knot closure or bead tip to the color of the clasp. Don't forget to use a karat gold bead tip with karat gold clasps. Or if fine gold tips are not available to you, use French wire instead, it will look much nicer.

Please remember, when using silk or nylon, to wash your hands thoroughly and keep a damp cloth nearby to wipe your fingers occasionally while stringing. The light colors show the slightest dirt and oil, and your beautiful necklace can be ruined if the cord is dirty or tattle-tale gray from sweaty fingers. Believe it or not, your fingers do perspire, especially during knotting. Oil from your skin will look very dark on a strand of white silk, so keep a damp cloth handy, and use it often.

USING FRENCH WIRE
(BULLION)

Take a length of silk and thread it through the needle eye and double the string, bringing the two ends together. DO NOT TIE THE ENDS. Using the needle, go through the first pearl, drawing the strand through, until you have a four inch tail leftover. Cut a half-inch length of bullion and thread it over the needle and onto the silk, bringing it to rest against the pearl. Remember, your strand is loose and any tension could cause the pearl to slip off the end. Now, go through the clasp ring and allow the clasp to slide down over the bullion.

Thread the needle back down through the pearl, pulling slightly so that the bullion gathers somewhat in front of the pearl. At this point, you should have a loop of French wire about three to four millimeters in diameter, attached to the clasp ring. The loose ends of the silk should now be tied to the strand in an overhand knot, a drop of glue applied and a second knot tied to form a square knot. DO NOT trim the tail. Allow it to dry while you finish the strand and then clip. The other end of the strand will be done the same way after the last pearl is added.

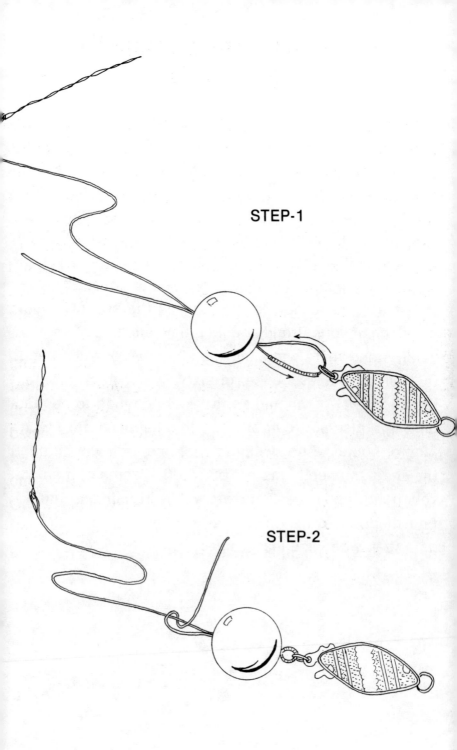

STEP-1

STEP-2

KNOTTING BETWEEN BEADS

Pearls and fine stone beads are knotted for three reasons. First and foremost, to prevent wear at the hole. The beads rubbing together on the strand, will eventually ruin the beads. They will flatten at the holes and look like the mouth of a volcano, after a while. Once the holes start wearing on pearls, the outer layer (nacre) will begin to peel away and the duller conchiolin layer will show, EVEN ON NATURAL (Oriental) pearls. When this occurs, you no longer have pearls, but dull, lifeless white beads.

The second reason for knotting is the security of the necklace. If your strand should break, and it isn't knotted, you'll stand there watching the sixty-five or more pearls fly, roll, ping and bounce, in sixty-five or more different directions. If you should be fortunate enough to be standing in a nice soft carpet when this happens, they won't ping or bounce. They will, instead, find their way through the shag and nestle there. You will find some of them, on your hands and knees. The rest will lie in wait, and you will find them, one at a time, after a months time, with your bare feet, when you least expect it.

Lastly, pearls are knotted for purely aesthetic reasons. With a knot in between each one, they aren't bunched up against each other and they drape better since they move more freely. Knots are NOT decorative. They should be only large enough so they won't slip into the drill hole. Use the heaviest silk you can for the beads, but not so heavy that it forms a big, ugly knot that just sits there looking obnoxious. They should just quietly and unobtrusively do their job.

Your first knotting job will have to be re-done after you finish. But that's to be expected. The first time is just for practice and to develop the rhythm of tying the knots. You will have gaps, with a bead here and a knot there, but that's alright. Get the feeling first. Then perfect it. Don't get discouraged. Go slow and keep trying. You can do it.

TYING THE KNOTS

Start the strand in the usual manner, using a bead tip, knot closure or the bullion to connect the clasp.

Loop the silk around the pearl so you have an open knot. Insert the awl or 'tee pin' into the loop and work it up as close as possible to the pearl. When the knot is snug against the pearl, pull the strand to tighten, working the knot into place, using the awl, or pin. Remove the awl, separate the two strings, just below the knot, and pull the strands away from each other, using just a little tension. This will encourage the knot closer to the pearl and tighten it as much as possible. Add another pearl to the strand pushing it tightly against the knot, loop the silk around into a loose knot, insert the awl and tighten. Separate the two strings and pull apart to work the knot snug against the pearl. Add another pearl pushing the knot hard and continue in this manner with succeding pearls, tying each one as you go, except for the last two pearls, if you are finishing with bullion. If you are using bead tips or knot closures, knot all the pearls, attach the bead tip or knot closure and attach the clasp. If you are using bullion, the last two pearls are left unknotted. Add

STEP-1

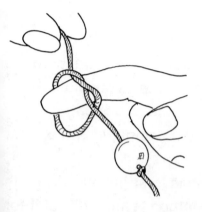

STEP-2

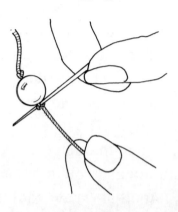

STEP-3

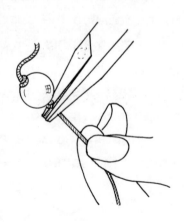

STEP-4

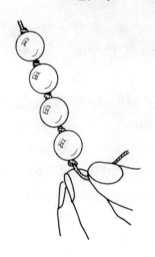

a half-inch length of French wire, go through the clasp ring, and back down through the last pearl to knot. Add a drop of glue. Go through the next pearl and knot again adding glue. Now go through the third bead and after drawing the strand all the way through the pearl, glue the string at the hole and clip it off as close as possible to the drill hole. The glue will keep the silk from working it's way back up through the pearl. Trim the beginning end of your strand and you're done.

Another way to knot the strand is to string all the pearls first, and then knot them. This method is more difficult for the beginner, so wait until you are comfortable tying the knots before trying this. This method seems to go more quickly, since you don't break the rhythm of tying to add another pearl.

Thread all the pearls onto the strand at once. Use a slip knot at the needle end of the strand to keep the pearls from slipping off. Let all the pearls remain at this end so they will be out of the way while you knot. Slide a pearl into place, tie the knot, then slide the next one into place and continue. You will use the awl to work the knot into place and separate the strands to tighten the knot as discussed before. Finishing the ends is the same.

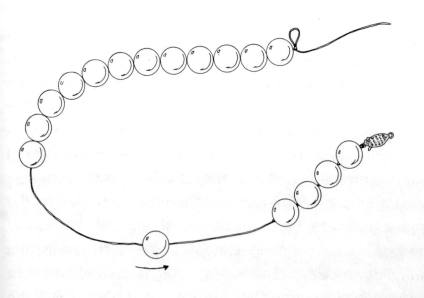

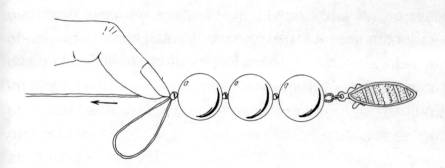

Once you've been knotting a while and you get comfortable doing it, you may want to try knotting without using the awl or pin. If you can master this, it will really cut down on the time it takes to knot a strand. Once again, it takes a lot of practice, but soon you'll be doing it without thinking.

Start in the usual way, adding the clasp. String all the pearls onto the strand and slide the first pearl into place. Bring a loop of silk up around the first pearl, pulling the loop to the side, tight. Place your thumbnail right under the loop, holding it snug against the pearl. Now draw the strand down away from the pearl. Your thumbnail will keep the knot in place and it will tighten right behind the pearl. Now separate the strings and pull away from each other to work the knot as close as possible to the pearl. Continue in this way until all the pearls are knotted. Do keep your awl or 'tee pin' close by, just in case you need to work a stubborn knot a little closer, or to take a knot out.

After a short time using this method, you'll find that you can tie knots without watching constantly, and it will go quickly.

DOUBLE NEEDLE METHOD

A somewhat more time consuming, but simpler way of knotting, is the double needle method. You use two needles and two single strands of silk. To form a single strand, if you are using silk from a spool, thread the silk through the needle about two inches, and leave the end free. You will have to be careful with this loose end, since it can pull right out of the needle, so don't use any tension on the needle. Thread both needles through the bead tip, knot closure or bullion, just as you would normally. Add the first pearl and tie an overhand knot, pulling the two strands taut to force the knot close against the pearl. Bring both needles together again to add the next pearl, separate the strand to tie an overhand knot and tighten. Continue adding a pearl and tying, until all the pearls are strung. Finish as you normally do with the bead tip or other ending.

This takes considerable time, and is a little more cumbersome, but if you need the knots placed exactly, and you are not quite sure of your ability, this works very well, even on your very first try.

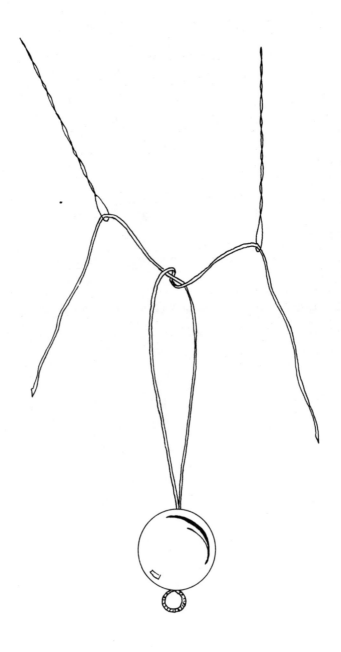

HAVING FUN WITH FANCY BEADS

Up till now, we've been working with only one strand at a time. Now that you have really mastered the stringing and knotting, we can move on to more complicated and fun necklaces, using twister strands, convertible necklaces, lariats, ropes and continous strands.

Let your imagination run freely, there is no right or wrong, just fashion and fun. You may want to add some shell, cloissone, fluted metal beads, tassels or just one special accent to the center front. Use contrasting colors and shapes for texture, or complimenting colors and finishes for a more conservative look. The only guidelines you need to follow, will be in the how-to of putting the strands together on the clasp. The rest is up to you.

You will need to add twister strand clasps, cones and multiple strand clasps to your inventory of beading supplies, in order to finish the necklaces professionally. These will be explained as we go along.

TWISTER STRANDS

Twister strands of small beads or pearls are a fun and colorful accent to your wardrobe. You may want to use freshwater rice pearls, in a rainbow of colors, either natural or dyed, or pearls and natural stone beads combined.

The strands are strung individually, like a single strand with one exception. The ends are left loose and are not attached to anything. Make a knot about four inches from the end. String the beads on the cord as you usually do either knotted or unknotted, as you prefer. After the last bead, make a knot to secure the strand and clip the end about four inches from the knot, leaving a tail. Set aside. Do the other strands in the same manner. When all the strands are completed, tie the tail of each strand, at one end, together so you have one big tail of six or eight strands. Glue the knot. Tie the opposite ends together to form another tail and glue. After the glue dries, trim some of the strands away so you don't have quite so many. Thread the remaining strands through a needle and bring them through the wide end of a cone and into a bead tip to knot. Add a drop of glue and dry. If you are using a twister clasp, go directly into the clasp and knot. Finish as usual doing the opposite end in the same manner.

TWISTER STRAND

CONVERTIBLE STRANDS

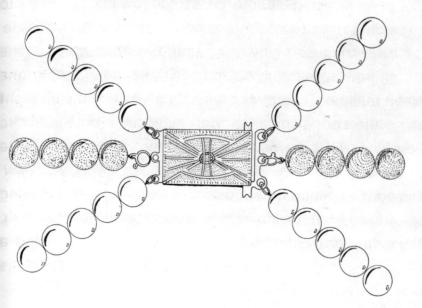

43

CONVERTIBLE MULTIPLE STRANDS

Multiple strand necklaces can be attached to a clasp having several rings, fastening one or two strands to each of the rings. They may have as many as seven rings attached. They can be worn flat, for a layered look, or twisted. An added bonus to this type of clasp is that you may add or remove strands very simply. Here's how you do it.

Select a three, five or seven strand clasp. String enough strands to attach to every other ring on the clasp. You may attach several strands to each ring if you like, depending on how heavy a necklace you like. You should now have one open ring in the center of a three row clasp, two open rings on a five strand, or three on a seven strand clasp.

Now, string as many contrasting strands as you like attaching a spring ring clasp to BOTH ends of the strand. When these are completed, you simply attach the strands using the spring rings, to the empty rings on the clasp. Now you will be able to change the strands at will, to match any color. Pearls (freshwater) work very well with this concept since white goes with all colors, and they can be dressed up or down for a sporty or formal look, depending on your mood.

SECTIONED MULTIPLE STRANDS

Another very pretty way to do beads or pearls, is a sectioned multiple strand necklace, having several strands of small beads, brought together at intervals with a single larger bead. Select the beads you want to use and lay them out on the bead board, arranging the pattern you want to use. Perhaps you would like to use three strands of 4mm rose quartz beads, brought together with a 10mm bead of garnet, at fifteen bead intervals.

String the first strand, starting as you normally do. Knotting between each bead is NOT recommended for this style necklace, but for security, you may want to knot at the large bead, however, this is done later. String the fifteen small beads (or the number needed for your pattern) then a large bead and so on, until the first strand is completed. Do NOT attach to the clasp. The second strand is started, using the bead tip or knot closure from the first strand. Add the small beads, bring the strand through the large bead on the first strand and separate again to add the next section of small beads. Continue this way until the second strand is completed. The third strand is done the same way. Bring all the strands together for knotting as one, and attach to the clasp as one strand. Knot only the large beads.

MULTIPLE
STRAND

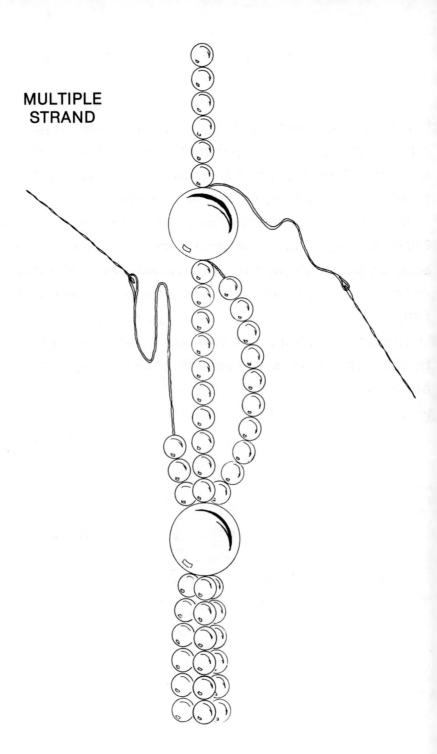

Now, you should have enough knowledge behind you, to put multiple strands together in many different ways. Basically, they are all done separately, then gathered together and fastened to the clasp as one.

All of these methods will allow you to either wear the beads twisted or layered. Remember, when you twist the strands, you don't want to twist excessively, or the whole necklace will twist around on itself where it falls in the front.

Try braiding strands or weaving. Experiment with the beads. You may be surprised with the new ways you can string them.

CONTINUOUS STRANDS

A continuous strand is a long strand of 26 inches or more, with no clasp, and slips right over the head. This is usually done when there is no front section or center decoration, and the pattern is uniform all the way around. You never have to worry about the clasp twisting around your neck to the front, or the clasp coming apart.

To do a continuous strand, follow your usual method, but do not use a bead tip or any other end, and do not attach to a clasp. If you are knotting the strand, DO NOT tie the first two beads, or the last two beads. Use a slip knot at the beginning of the strand to keep the beads from slipping off. After all the beads are on the strand, run the string through the first bead and pull snug. Tie a square knot onto the strand with the tail and glue. Thread the string through the next bead, tie and glue again. Allow to dry. Pull the slip knot from the other tail (beginning end) and thread it into the needle. Run the strand through the last bead, tie a square knot and glue. Repeat with the next bead. Now you have two strands crossed over each other in the four beads that come together. When the glue has dried trim tails as close as possible to the drill holes.

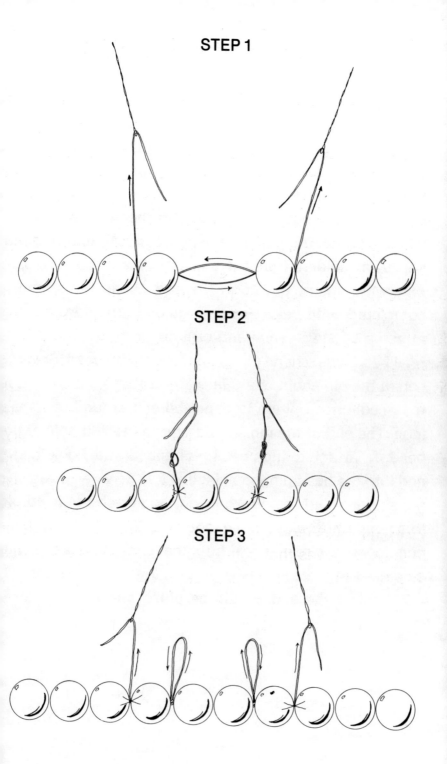

STEP 1

STEP 2

STEP 3

LARIATS

Lariats are long strands that don't connect at the ends to form a necklace. The ends are left loose to tie in a square knot, or held together with a clip or shortener, with the ends left to dangle freely. Most lariats are 36 inches or longer.

The procedure is the same as for other strands, but you will not attach a clasp. Use bead tips or a jump ring that has been soldered shut if you want to attach a tassel, otherwise a knot will be at the end. When the strand is completed, with bead tips or rings on both ends, you can attach a tassle to each end or a single bead. To add the final bead, use a head pin to go through the bead. Snip the end of the pin about one-quarter inch above the bead. Use the needle nose pliers to bend the end around to form a loop. The end of the pin should fit into the drill hole of the bead. To attach to the bead tip on the strand, hook the tip end into the head pin loop just like you do when attaching a clasp and curl the hook closed. To attach the head pin to a jump ring, twist the pin loop away from itself, without opening the circle, hook into the jump ring and twist closed.

A knot at the end should be glued and trimmed after drying.

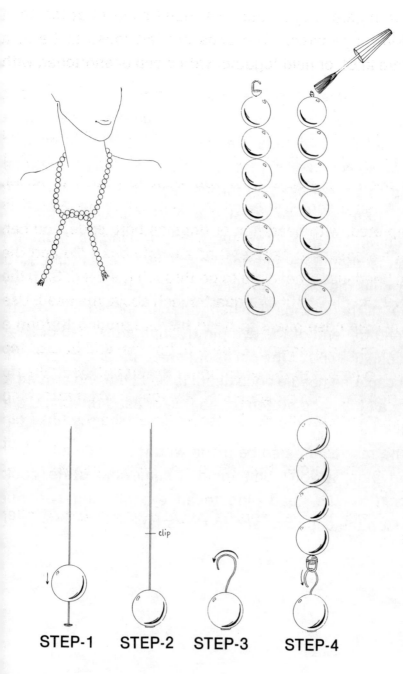

STEP-1   STEP-2   STEP-3   STEP-4

clip

TASSELS

Tassels are used to add a decorative end to lariats and sometimes to the center of other necklaces. They are made up of several short strands of tiny beads or even chain, gathered at one end in a bell cap or fancy shaped bead. Let your imagination be your guide on this and have fun. As a rule of thumb, use more contrast and variety for a casual look and less for a more conservative appearance. Tassels are not used on formal necklaces.

To form a tassel on silk, use your usual method of stringing, starting with a jump ring or bead tip. Make the strands about one and one-half or two inches long. Knot and glue the last bead and trim after drying. When you have all the strands finished, attach them to an eye pin. Thread the end of the eye pin through a bell cap or bead and clip the end of the pin about one-quarter inch past the bell cap. Use needle nose pliers to bend the end around to form a circle and attach to the ring or bead tip on the end of the lariat.

The tassle can also be made with the beads strung on head pins, if you don't mind a somewhat stiffer look. Attach all the head pins to an eye pin and continue through the cap to attach to the lariat.

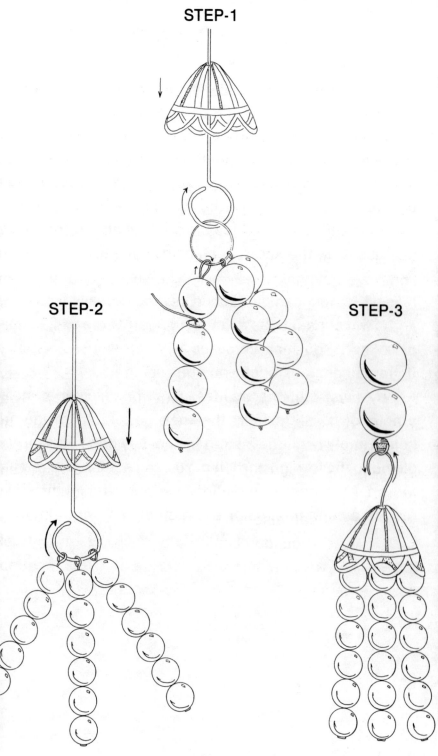

STEP-1

STEP-2

STEP-3

TRADE SECRETS

A little known trade secret is white pearl fingernail polish. Use it on real pearls, or simulated, for touchups to discolored or peeling pearls. After cleaning pearls, if a few stubborn stains remain, paint them with a couple of light coats of enamel. Pearls that have begun to peel or flake, can be protected from further peeling, with several coats and the pearl color will hide the damage already done. You can use it on the knots in place of glue, especially if the knots are obvious. The knot at the end of a lariat, or the tassel strands, can be dabbed several times with enamel, and it will appear to be a tiny seed pearl at the end, instead of a knot. You may come up with other uses for pearl fingernail enamel, once you start using it.

Tiny, twist-drill bits are lifesavers when glue dries inside a hole, or if silk (usually the knot) gets stuck in the drill hole. Simply twist the bit into the hole by hand and you will dislodge the foreign particles. You can sometimes re-align the hole for easier threading. Serious re-alignment will require a hand tool, such as jewelers use, with a motor.

You should, by now, be well on your way to stringing beads to your heart's content. It is our sincere hope that most of your questions have been answered and we made the instructions clear enough for you to follow, successfully.

If you should discover new ways to string beads, or have suggestions to make stringing easier or less time consuming, we are anxious to hear from you.

Every effort has been made to help you get started with this handbook. If you feel we have overlooked something or did not explain clearly, your constructive criticism will be welcomed.

Letters should be addressed to me, in care of the publisher.

SOME DO'S AND DON'TS

NEVER force a needle or cord through a bead. Use a
smaller size.

Do not use crimp beads on silk or nylon. They are recommended for tiger tail/monofilament only.

Do not use 'super' type glues. White glue is best, it keeps
the strand flexible.

Do not try to squeeze a bead tip closed. Roll the hook
closed.

Do stretch nylon or twisted cord before finishing the
strand or knotting.

Do pull knots as tight as possible to the bead.

When disassembling a strand, remove beads one at a time
for restringing and work over a box or bead board
to catch loose beads.

NEVER soak simulated pearls in anything. The finish will
loosen and peel.

NEVER use alcohol, acetone or acids on cultured or
natural pearls to remove glue.

Do use a household cement to stiffen silk or nylon cord if
the needle should break off and you need a
temporary needle to finish.

Austrian Crystal and other glass beads, have very sharp
drill holes, which can cut through silk or nylon
cord. For this reason, we suggest tiger tail for the
job and forego knotting.

HOW MANY BEADS PER INCH

BEAD SIZE (millimeters)	APPROXIMATE COUNT
1 mm	25
2 mm	12.5
3 mm	8.3
4 mm	6.25
5 mm	5
6 mm	4
7 mm	3.5
8 mm	3
9 mm	2.75
10 mm	2.5
11 mm	2.25
12 mm	2
13 mm	1.9
14 mm	1.75
15 mm	1.6

WHERE TO FIND BEAD SUPPLIES

SILK/NYLON: Jewelry supply or findings store.

MONOFILAMENT: Bait and tackle (fishing) shop.

TIGER TAIL: (also called 'Leader Material') Jewelry supply or bait and tackle store.

BEADING NEEDLES: Jewelry supply or findings house.

CRIMP BEADS/BEAD TIPS/KNOT CLOSURES/FRENCH WIRE/CLASPS: Jewelry supply or findings store.

AWL/TWEEZERS/HEAD LOUPE/BEADING BOARDS: Jewelry supply or findings house.

NEEDLE NOSE PLIERS: Jewelry supply or hardware store

CONES/BELL CAPS/HEAD OR EYE PINS: Jewelry supply findings house.

COST OF SUPPLIES

SILK/NYLON: On cards - $1.00 to $2.00 each.
Spools: $10 - $15 for silk, $5 - $10 for nylon

MONOFILAMENT/TIGER TAIL: $2.00 to $3.00 (pack of 30 ft.)

NEEDLES: 59¢ to $1.00 each.

CRIMP BEADS/BEAD TIPS/KNOT CLOSURES: 10¢ to 25¢ each or $1.00 - $2.00 for karat gold.

FRENCH WIRE (bullion) $1.00 - $2.00 per foot.

HEAD LOUPE: $25 to $35.

PLIERS: $10 to $25 depending on quality.

HEAD/EYE PINS: 10¢ each.